THE GREAT OUTDOORS
CAMPING

By Adeline Snyder

Gareth Stevens
Publishing

Please visit our website, www.garethstevens.com. For a free color catalog of all our high-quality books, call toll free 1-800-542-2595 or fax 1-877-542-2596.

Library of Congress Cataloging-in-Publication Data

Snyder, Adeline.
Camping / Adeline Snyder.
    p. cm. — (The great outdoors)
Includes index.
ISBN 978-1-4339-7088-7 (pbk.)
ISBN 978-1-4339-7089-4 (6-pack)
ISBN 978-1-4339-7087-0 (library binding)
1. Camping I. Title.
GV191.7.S649 2013
796.54—dc23

2011045635

First Edition

Published in 2013 by
Gareth Stevens Publishing
111 East 14th Street, Suite 349
New York, NY 10003

Copyright © 2013 Gareth Stevens Publishing

Designer: Michael J. Flynn
Editor: Therese Shea

Photo credits: Cover, p. 1 © iStockphoto.com/Robert Churchill; p. 5 SNEHIT/Shutterstock.com; p. 5 (inset) Adisa/Shutterstock.com; p. 6 savenkov/Shutterstock.com; p. 9 AISPIX/Shutterstock.com; p. 10 Gorilla/Shutterstock.com; p. 13 Mat Hayward/Shutterstock.com; pp. 14, 15 Nate A./Shutterstock.com; p. 17 Golden Pixels LLC/Shutterstock.com, p. 18 Francois Arseneault/Shutterstock.com; p. 19 Sasha Burkard/Shutterstock.com; p. 20 Morgan Lane Photography/Shutterstock.com.

Printed in the United States of America

CPSIA compliance information: Batch #CS12GS: For further information contact Gareth Stevens, New York, New York at 1-800-542-2595.

CONTENTS

Words in the glossary appear in **bold** type the first time they are used in the text.

THE GREAT ESCAPE

BEEP! "Watch out!" *HONK HONK!* "Hurry up!" Many people like to escape the loud noise and fast pace of their lives. They may travel to a more natural setting, such as a national park. Sometimes, people stay overnight and camp there.

Instead of waking up to an alarm clock buzzing, campers wake to birds chirping. Rather than being surrounded by skyscrapers, campers may be surrounded by trees. Camping offers all this—and adventure, too!

INTO THE WILD

More than 3 million people visited Yellowstone National Park in the summer of 2011.

When you're camping in a national park, it's easy to forget the noise and crowds of city life.

5

INTO THE WILD

The largest national park is in Alaska. The Wrangell–St. Elias National Park and Preserve covers 13.2 million acres!

Some campgrounds are near the ocean. Others are in the desert. Some people like to camp in the mountains during winter!

WHERE TO CAMP

Campers need to find a campground first. Campgrounds may be public or private. National parks, national forests, and state and local parks often have public campgrounds. The government **maintains** these lands. Private campgrounds are owned and maintained by businesses or private citizens. Campers usually pay to use both public and private campgrounds.

All campgrounds are different. Some provide bathrooms, showers, and water fountains. Some have special areas where campers can safely build fires and use grills to cook food. Others don't have any of these things, so campers really "rough it"!

DO YOUR HOMEWORK!

Campers should find out as much as possible about a campground before their trip. Many campgrounds have websites where campers can learn more about them. Different kinds of activities may be offered, such as fishing, swimming, or horseback riding. Campers should check the weather at the campground, too. In some places, the weather can be very warm during the day but quite cold at night.

Campers can also find out if they need to make a **reservation**. Many campgrounds become crowded at certain times of the year.

Campers need to pack wisely. Many campgrounds are very far from stores.

TENT CAMPING

Some people like to camp in comfortable conditions, so they travel in **recreational vehicles** (RVs) or rent cabins. However, many others like tent camping.

A good tent can **protect** campers from rain, sun, and wind. A waterproof covering called a rainfly keeps bad weather out. A tent should also have **vents** that let air in and out. Even the smallest tent must have strong poles that won't bend easily. It's always a good idea for campers to practice setting up their tent before they go camping.

INTO THE WILD

Tents come in many shapes.
Dome tents are the most popular
for all weather conditions.

11

SLEEPING GEAR

Camping often involves a lot of tiring activities such as hiking and swimming. Campers need a comfortable place to sleep if they're tent camping. Many rest in a sleeping bag at night. On hard ground, a pad can be placed under the sleeping bag for some extra softness. Some pads protect the camper if the ground is cold or wet, too.

Cots are another way to make a camper's bed more comfortable. A cot keeps a camper off the ground. However, cots can be heavy. Some campers like to pack only what they can carry.

12

Some kinds of sleeping bags are meant for people sleeping in very cold or wet places. Most campers don't need these expensive supplies.

13

Some campers prefer to build a fire to cook their food rather than use a grill.

14

COOKING OUT

Cooking over a fire is one of the best parts of camping! At many campgrounds, visitors can bring **charcoal** and a lighter and be ready to cook in minutes. Special pots are best for high heat, but a hot dog cooked on a stick works well, too!

Campers should keep food in coolers or tightly shut bags. They don't want to draw animals to their campsite. In areas with bears, some people tie their food in a bag and hang it in a tree away from their tent.

INTO THE WILD

The **recipe** for s'mores – the graham cracker, marshmallow, and chocolate treat – was first published in 1927 in a Girl Scout handbook.

CAMPING ACTIVITIES

Camping activities are different at each campground. If there's a lake, river, or ocean nearby, campers may be able to swim or use a **kayak**. Fishing sometimes requires a **permit**. In most campgrounds, there are trails for hiking.

Hiking is an excellent way to see many kinds of plants and animals. Most campsites have trail maps so campers can get the most out of their hike and, more importantly, don't get lost. Some people hike with all their camping gear in backpacks!

INTO THE WILD

Campers honor the saying "leave no trace," which means to leave a place exactly as it's found. They never litter or harm wildlife or plants.

Hiking is good exercise — and it's fun, too!

Campers should pay close attention to campground signs. This sign warns campers to be careful of fire due to hot, dry weather.

LOW MODERATE HIGH EXTREME

FIRE DANGER

SUSTAINABLE RESOURCE DEVELOPMENT

SAFE ADVENTURES

Camping is about having fun, but campers should always keep in mind that they're in the wilderness. There are a few simple rules to keep campers safe and to protect the campground for others.

- Be sure to stay with at least one adult at all times.
- Keep to trails and paths set up by the campground.
- Wild animals are exactly that—wild—so don't feed them or get too close.
- Only adults should prepare campfires. The fires should be put out after use.

BEAR COUNTRY
Store all food in vehicle
Read bulletin board regulations
All wildlife are dangerous.

REGISTER
BEFORE
ENTERING
CAMPGROUND

READY, SET, CAMP!

Camping is about spending time with family and friends. It's about seeing countless stars in the sky. It's about sitting around a campfire laughing, singing, and telling stories. Every camping trip is an event to remember.

If you think you're interested in camping, you might want to try camping in your backyard first. Sometimes community parks invite people to camp there, too. Hopefully, you'll get a chance to admire nature—and feel grateful for the comfort of your own home! Are *you* ready for a camping adventure?

IMPORTANT CAMPING SUPPLIES

- tent
- knife
- sleeping bag
- flashlight
- first-aid kit
- insect spray
- clean water
- whistle
- food
- trash bags
- rope
- compass

21

GLOSSARY

charcoal: a type of fuel, often made from wood, that is used for cooking

dome: a rounded roof

kayak: a lightweight boat, often for one person, that moves by paddling

maintain: to care for something by making repairs and changes when needed

permit: a printed document from a government or organization that allows someone to own or do something

preserve: a place set aside for animals and plants

protect: to guard

recipe: an explanation of how to make food

recreational vehicle: a type of car with spaces for sleeping and eating. Also called an RV or motor home.

reservation: a way of saving a space

trace: a sign that remains after someone or something leaves a place

vent: a small opening that allows air in and out

FOR MORE INFORMATION

BOOKS

Douglas, Ed, and Kate Douglas. *Camping.* New York, NY: DK Publishing, 2009.

Klein, Adam G. *Camping.* Edina, MN: ABDO Publishing, 2008.

WEBSITES

Great American Backyard Campout
online.nwf.org/site/PageNavigator/gabc_2010_home
Find out about this annual backyard camping event.

Recreation.gov
www.recreation.gov
Research campsites all across the country.

WebRangers
www.nps.gov/webrangers/
Learn about the national parks while playing games.

INDEX